DEAR FUTURE ANNA

DEAR FUTURE ANNA

ANNA-LIESE PRINCE

Icons Media Publishing

This book is dedicated to both children and adults.

With love,
Anna-liese Prince.

About The Author

My name is Anna-liese Prince and I'm the author of this book. This is the second book that I've written, but I love it just as much. You as a reader only know me as an author, the person that wrote this book, but I'm so much more than that, and this page will help you to understand who I really am, and the reason why I've written this book; the reason why I've chosen to be an author.

Months after I wrote my first book, I began to realise my responsibilities. I was training for my exams for secondary school, and I came across a diary that was perfect to write in. At first, I was just writing poems, random things that I thought had no meaning, but when my mother came across what I wrote, she knew that I had the special ability to write, well, she had always known, but once again, it took me a little longer to realise. She created a page for me on Microsoft word and encouraged me to type up the poems that I had previously written. I then began to realise that what I was writing wasn't just a fabrication of how my young mind worked, but it was in fact the truth, different experiences that was embedded in my mind, almost as if I was on this earth before. I was writing things that I never knew that I was capable of writing, and that was how I started to write again.

Meanwhile at school, every break time or lunchtime, I chose to write poems, it was things that I thought of and wrote down, I thought it wasn't good enough, but when I truly read and edited it, I began to believe that I was able to do it, that I could write another book. Every time I couldn't think of ideas, I asked my encouraging mother for just a word, or maybe even a sentence, we would sit down for a few minutes discussing different titles, and this encouraged me to write a little more; she too believed that I could do it. I began to write almost every day, going on word and editing it as much as I could, it took a while for everything to come together. I thought that fifty poems was too long, but my mother believed that I could do it, even though I didn't believe in myself.

After writing so many poems, I began to lose ideas, I didn't know what else I could write about. I procrastinated so I didn't have to write the book, making excuses that I knew weren't true. That changed when my mother made me write poetry ideas, she helped me to know that I could do better, helped me to know that I was not at my true potential. I began to write again, ticking off each poem as I did. I was so happy that she believed in me, and I knew that she was truly proud of me.

It was winter half term when I truly saw the greatness of my capabilities. I was beginning to do six or seven poems every day, and day after day, I realised that my potential for writing was flourishing; and as I approached the last poem, my mother knew that this poem was going to be special for me, and that it should be special for my readers too. I'm thankful that she helped me to both write and edit my work, making me understand that everyone made mistakes, and what I could improve on. She is the best person in my life, and I'm truly grateful for that. She is not the only one that helped me to believe that I can continue to write, but I will always love her until the day I die.

To the people that inspired me to carry on with my career in writing, even if it was a few kind words: My Mother, Father, Mrs Ayling, Mrs Ashby and Nandita.

The people that aren't included in this list may not have helped me with this book, but they helped to make me believe that I can do anything I wanted, as long as I put my mind to it. They also comforted me when I was sad. You may not be here, but I will never forget you.

Published by Icons Media Publishing in 2023

My Future Self

Time: 19:10
Date: 10/2/2022

Dear future me, what do you see?
As your past life is my life,
The things you love would have changed,
I am embedded in the body of a pandemic,
I can't even get out,
But now that you are stronger, you can overcome even my fears,
I thought that I was versatile, but you're the alpha.

~

The way that I feel, may be so much more different than you,
What I see, would be so much different than what you see,
I understand the meaning to life, but you will understand so
much more.

~

I feel, hear, see, smell, and taste my future, and that is you,
My wishes are to be a doctor and you will face that head on,
I may be a child, and you may be an adult,
But the things that I love, that are truly important to me,
Should be the same as yours,
As we together, are one.

Don't send me to the moon,
Don't send me to the stars,
Just send me to the sunshine,
Forget about Mars.

~

I want to sleep in the sunshine,
As the sun ripples through my clothes,
Streaming deep within my blood,
As I'm watching life grow cold.

~

I taste the bitter taste of death,
The bittersweet taste of sadness,
I see the way that the heinous actions of humans affect the lives
of others,
Our world has turned into a place of darkness,
But yet, as I'm lying down in the sun, I can feel its sharpness.

~

I can see the arrays of sunshine glimmering across the sky,
Overcoming this time of dread,
As its yellows and oranges reflect across our land,
It feel like in our darkest ages it came to lend a hand,

Our lives can't live without it, with sunlight our human race can stand.

Equality
Time: 15:59
Date: 16/2/2022

Equality isn't about the colour of your skin,
But the importance of everyone in the human race,
Even if you are a boy or a girl,
Liking or not liking someone,
It's important that everyone feels that they are equal,
It's not just about differences, we can all be the same at heart.

~

We describe people as their differences, the thing that makes
them special,
We all are different, and that shouldn't change a thing,
So, when we're sick or short, why are we classified as different?
The importance of our differences are the things that give us
classification.

~

When we're different we're special, and isn't that important?
We believe the things that aren't always true,
And that affects us tremendously,
What's the point in being rude?
Because I know you wouldn't like it, if someone did it to you.

Thank you for the world,
Thank you for my eyes,
Thank you for my hands and fingers,
Thank you for my life,
These are the words that expose the world of strife.

~

Thank you for the stars, the moon, and the sun,
The things that make our human race feel like they've won.

~

It's not easy to accept the horrible people that are our race,
They make us feel like our whole life is some kind of chase.

~

Accepting our life sounds like some kind of joke,
And that this world feels like it's making you choke,
Although our world of sadness sound like a game,
There is always some sunshine in this world of blame.

~

After so many weeks, after so many months,
It may seem like it's not getting better,

There's always going to be something good, like a nice love letter.

~

Our world of depression can be a lot sweeter,
If we appreciated the important things in our lives,
And when you really see the good things in our world,
You'd have the bitter-sweet taste of thankfulness.

Beginnings
Time: 17:48
Date: 28/2/2022

The beginning of growth,
The beginning of the construction of a building,
The beginning of a year when everyone cheers.
The experience it can create, can be as extraordinary as its
ending,
But it isn't always the greatest, like the beginning of a war.

~

The beginning of a trend,
The beginning of a friendship,
The things that make us whole can be taken away in an instant.

~

Beginnings may be horrible, but sometimes it's the ending that
counts,
Like the beginning of pregnancy, pain and moaning,
And the ending of a birth, cheering and tears of joy.

~

We can blame and make excuses,
We can cry and we can pout,
But instead, we should try and then we'll succeed,
Because the beginning of our journey is very important,
But don't allow that to be the reason of procrastination.

Sanity
Time: 18:24
Date: 10/2/2022

It is always important to maintain our **sanity**,
As life can under mind us and overpower us with **vanity**.
Vanity you say, yes, it can mean having too much pride,
We take and take, as we stand by and watch love slide.

~

*But let's stop for a minute and talk about **humanity**,*
We leave the poor to die young, as we drown our sins and pretend
*like we believe in **Christianity**.*
Maintaining your sanity is all about giving, your mental health,
and respecting your religion.

~

Now that we've talked about sanity and humanity, let's talk
about **profanity**.
You could swear, you could shout, you could even kick and run
about,
But what we need to learn, is that we can always back out.

~

Why make life so hard? When all we need to do is respect the
people that we love,
And we can finally see, how our actions affect their sanity, not
just ours.

Fruits
<u>Time: 19:08</u>
<u>Date: 16/11/2021</u>

Fruits are very neat,
But they are also big, small, short, long, enormous and petite,
It is just great for a treat!
Green, purple, brown, orange, yellow and sweet.

~

Apples are round,
They are seen half eaten and splattered on the rock-hard ground,
Bananas are curved,
Cake, bread, ice cream, milkshakes, yes, these are the meals that
are included when served.

~

Let's talk about berries,
There are elderberries, cloudberries, huckleberries, gooseberries,
strawberries, blackberries, and blueberries.
Blueberries are sweet, small, blue, and healthy,
Their energy is used to make us beautifully wealthy.

~

Oranges are hard because of its outside peeling,
But it's the inside of it that makes it worth concealing,
Thieves might even think that it's even worth stealing,
But when it squeezes in their eye, it is not a nice feeling.

~

Now, let's talk about pears.
Most people think that this tastes like hair,
But that's something we shouldn't even compare,
But we are all young, so we don't even care!
And that's the reason we need to realise that we should be
thankful that it's even there.

~

The point of the matter is, there are some amazing fruits!
Now you can proudly read this like you are wearing a new suit
and boots,
This is the reason that we should love our roots,
Because all over the world, there are all different kinds of fruits.

Love
Time: 19:42
Date: 18/11/2021

Love is like a cloud,
It just drifts and drifts without a reason,
It can stab us in the heart, making us love and care for others.
Or even trap us in a permanent cage of love, which we cannot
escape.

~

Without love we're incomplete,
We just can't live without it,
We can live with love until our demise,
As love is beautiful and we should always have it,
Even when we're long, short, old, and young.

~

When love traps us in its own cage,
We feel that we can never get out,
Because love is something that will live with us forever.
And we will always remember our love together.

My Normal
Time: 18:05
Date: 15/2/2022

What I experience, could be so different than you,
The life that I'm living, could seem weird or strange,
But it's my normal, and normal can be different to many.

~

After so many years of being on this earth,
The things that I find important may seem so futile,
My understanding of the world always improves,
And old fears become my life.

~

So many things are now old and useless,
And new fears are brewing,
I thought I had overcome the things that I found difficult,
But life proved me wrong,
So many times, I feel defeated,
But in my life, it has become, my normal.

Life & Destruction
Time: 19:52
Date: 18/11/2021

Life is something that births like a mother,
Whereas destruction is the thing that destroys,
But although they're so different, they are very much alike,
They make beautiful things blossom.

~

They make beautiful things just like us, earth, and the solar
system,
And even when something can be so terrible, life can be made
from it.
So, when we die, something can grow and emerge from the
depths of darkness, and bloom into a gorgeous flower,
We hope that they will grow just like us, but we can always be
wrong.

~

Destruction destroys, manipulates, and imprisons,
You may even blame it for the life we're living in right now.
Death, carnage, bullies, and murderers,
The things and people that we cannot control,
We make it worse by hurting, killing, and bullying,
And watch as our life burns into darkness.

~

Life blooms every hour, minute and second,
It makes us who we are every day,
Babies, animals, you can name them all,
And life will emerge and take its role,
Allowing us to love its beautiful creation.

~

Like I said they're both so amazing together,
But we'll need to treat them better,
Because we always take it for granted, even when we know we
shouldn't.
This poem won't stop anyone from doing the things they
shouldn't do,
But we should always try, even if we don't succeed.

Dreams
Time: 19:55
Date: 14/11/2021

Dreams are the best,
Even the ones that make you over stress,
Sometimes, you want to put it to the test,
Some will make your heart pump out of your chest,
It could even be about a quest.

~

Or, it could be a recurring pest,
You just want to lay down, and get some rest,
It could be something you hate, or abhor, NO! Detest,
It could be something you have never guessed.

~

Some dreams might make you have a nightmare,
Like someone is holding you down, and blocking your access to
air,
It may be something you can't even bare,
But always remember, that your parents care,
Even if they're having an adulterous affair,
And even then, happiness isn't something you can wear.

Death
Time: 19:05
Date: 22/11/2021

Death is something we will always see at some point in our lives,
Because there is no such thing as living forever,
We all know that we will die someday,
But still, we waste our lives, doing nothing.

~

Everyone says that it impacts the family the most,
Yes, the father, the mother, and the children,
Sometimes people forget about the friends,
But they're still important before and after our deaths.

~

Everyone's sad, guilty, and mournful,
They think they could've done something to stop it from
happening,
That they could've done something to stop them dying,
But in the end, death is always meant to be,
Even if you will never see or understand it that way.

Teachers
Time: 18:56
Date: 23/11/2021

They teach, support, and care for us,
As they teach us life lessons, even when they are angry, they
never curse.
Teachers do not get the minimum wage,
And they do this for every single number of age.

~

They make us learn so much,
And you could say they did it even better, when we were kids
and we couldn't flush.

~

You may remember when you was young,
That the teachers made everything better, even when you bit the
tip of your tongue,
They made you learn such wonderful things,
Just enough so that you could spread your wings.

~

The point of this poem is that you should appreciate the people
that teach you,
Because even if you think you do,
It may not seem that way from their point of view,
And let's just hope that this is something you already knew,
Because this shouldn't be something that's new.

Knowledge
Time: 18:02
Date: 24/11/2021

The mind works amazingly,
Accordingly, and impressively,
And knowledge accommodates it,
Let's get comfy and sit,
While you read the best bits.

~

We all like to learn,
Even if that's football or dancing, it's something you have to
earn,
It could affect your life,
And make your world full of strife.

~

I would like to say,
That knowledge is something you can learn every day,
You have to work for your success,
And I had to learn that it wasn't something that you should
stress,

~

Because to be successful, you have to grow, learn and observe,
And trust me when I say, you will gain everything that you
deserve.

Earth
Time: 18:38
Date: 1/12/2021

Earth contains such amazing things,
There are things like friends, family, and wedding rings,
But we know that not all things are great that our world brings.

~

There are things like bullies, criminals, divorces, and death,
And sometimes they hurt everything and everyone with a single breath,
Yes, they are horrible and disgusting, yes, they really are,
But they don't affect humanity as much as cars.

~

Then there are things that conquer the bad,
And make children feel safe and glad,
Because they destroy the beast of this world,
I'm talking about the deep-rooted issues that makes your stomach twirl.

~

There are things like food, family, and friends,
That make you love them until your world ends,
But the easiest things can ruin such happy things,
Because we can all be horrible to everything our world brings.

Hate
<u>Time: 19:01</u>
<u>Date: 1/12/2021</u>

Hate has many traits,
As it soaks into the earth and into our bodies,
It can be shown in different ways,
But we all know that it's all the same thing.

~

It could be online, or in real life,
It could affect you in so many different ways,
Just like in the horror story of death.

~

It could be on social media,
A gaming app on your phone,
You could take a picture and in the comments there it lay,
There's so many things we could do to make this better,
But it isn't something you care about if it doesn't happen to
you.

Sadness
Time: 19:19
Date: 1/12/2021

Happiness isn't something we always feel,
Unfortunately, sadness is the alternative,
When it comes to sadness you may be their number one victim,
The slightest things may get you to cry,
Or maybe even in the inside.

~

Sometimes it could just be a word,
But even then, that could rub you the wrong way,
It could be an action, even if it's good or bad,
It could make salty tears stream down your face.

~

You may feel sadness, anger or even both,
But just remember that even when you are sad,
There's people to support you,
I may not be able to name all of them, but you know,
And if not, you just need to know that you are not alone.

Happiness
Time: 19:24
Date: 1/1/2022

Happiness is something we may not always feel,
In your darkest moments it may not even feel real,
And when you have so many emotions, it's so hard to conceal,
When this happens, you need to make yourself think that it's
the real deal.

~

There's so much to give, and hardly anything to get,
And people believe that happiness is a threat,
That may be true, happiness isn't a personal pet,
And sadly, the real world is full of threat.

~

This is called sadness, our menace, our enemy,
For this you may think there is no remedy,
We all have experienced it, it's our destiny,
But there's always something to help, like a little melody.

It illuminates the sky,
It's the thing that gives us night and rises up so very high,
It's so beautiful, that's how it seems to the naked eye,
But we should know how important it is, as the hours go by.

~

The night put almost everyone to sleep,
As they dream about counting sheep,
In the morning they remember what happened when they were
out in the deep,
But sometimes when they try, they begin to weep.

~

They remember a nightmare,
And try to get it out of their hair,
Sometimes it's too hard to bear,
And it's so horrible, that sleeping is so very rare.

~

They don't know why it's happening,
And to others it's baffling,
Maybe because they're babbling,
But sooner or later they will know what they're handling.

Authors
Time: 20:09
Date: 1/1/2022

Authors are great, as I am one too,
And sometimes it might look easy, but you have no clue,
Because you only care about writing that book, don't you?

~

I love books, they're so very interesting,
I love to think about what the author is thinking,
Even when I'm not listening.

~

It's so nice to write,
And my imagination won't go without a fight.
I don't like those simple books, like the princess and the knight,
Writing's so easy, it's like flying a kite,
And it doesn't even matter if you're smart, brainy or bright,
Because reading and writing, is such a delight.

Money

Money is the thing that keeps the world spinning,
But sadly, that's a contest that some of us aren't winning,
But there's more to it, this is just the beginning,

~

People say that money is just an object,
But how can they explain its effect?
When the actions people make just because it's something they collect?

~

Maybe it's just because it's so manipulating,
When people act like its money they are dating,
But do they understand that an object with a ripple effect isn't worth paying?

Parents
<u>Time: 14:26</u>
<u>Date: 4/1/2022</u>

Being a parent is a very important job,
As it's not about being a slob,
And you have to care about you child, even more so when they sob.

~

Parents play a huge role in children's lives,
As you need to protect them, from things like a knife,
And it has to be a full commitment, not just about being a wife.

~

If your child is hurt, you would feel the pain,
But learning to protect your child, isn't about financial gain,
It has to immediately resonates deep within you,
To live, protect, yes you have to use your brain,
Because the love for your child is what lives within you, like a stain.

The Ending
Time: 17:55
Date: 27/1/2022

An end,
The thing that will always happen.

~

Maybe it's a life,
Maybe it's a year,
Maybe it's a birth,
Maybe even a friendship.

~

You may be sad,
Or you may just not care,
But you'll always remember it,
Just like in the beginning.

~

After a while,
You'd think you wouldn't care,
You'd think it wouldn't matter,
But an ending affects us all so very differently,
But one thing is for sure,
Some of us might even find ourselves breaking down, instantly.

Invisibility
Time: 18:08
Date: 27/1/2022

If you were invisible, what would you do?
Would you walk around with everyone unable to see you?
Maybe you would act like a clown,
Play around and be really funny,
Jump around on the monkey bars, and act like a bunny.

~

Or maybe you would rob a bank,
Get some more money,
Buy some fishes and a fish tank,
Or visit the bees and eat up all their honey.

~

Maybe you wouldn't care,
Just sit around all day watching TV,
Crying in despair,
Or maybe laugh with glee.

~

Would you feel bad?
Sometimes very lonely,
You'd probably wouldn't eat, because you wanted to be some-
one's one and only,

~

Would you cry on the inside?
Because your life is now filled with lies,
After all this invisibility, you now feel that nobody would care if
you died.

Trying Your Best
<u>Time: 15:42</u>
<u>Date: 10/1/2022</u>

Trying your best,
Can sometimes be a test,
It can hurt so much; you'll end up feeling depressed.

~

You try and try,
But sometimes in the end you'll cry,
Your brain makes you think all those thoughts,
And it races through your mind, like some kind of sport.

~

To you, this may just look like a page of rhymes,
But I know trying takes time.
If you push and push, you may just get the right results,
And then you'll encourage other people, go ahead, act like it's a cult.

~

Because it's the result that matters,
And then you'll feel like you're shining like firecrackers.

Colours
Time: 15:46
Date: 30/1/2022

Colours are interesting,
Just like a song,
Maybe it's bright like the sun,
Or soft like a cushion,
Do you have a favourite?
Is it one or two?
Does colours make you happy?
Is it a nice colour?
To me, not all colours are nice and bright.

~

Red means angry, furious, and mad,
Green means disgusting, horrible and wretched,
Blue means sad, depressed, and gloomy,
And brown is dark, rotten and ugly.

~

That's if you look at colours in a dry and dull way,
So, let's try this again.
Red can mean romantic, green allows you to visualise the
colours of the earth,
Blue can stand as the colours of the sky, or the reflection of the
deep blue sea,
And brown, well, I don't know about that one.

~

Not all colours are sad and blue,
But not all colours are bright and exciting,
Maybe they're all equally nice, to you or to me,
But there's always a stereotype, but colours can sometimes grab
you by the neck.

The Ocean
Time: 16:57
Date: 30/1/2022

The ocean, a mystical place,
Filled with majestic creatures,
Big, small, short, tall,
There is such gratitude within their wonderful features.

~

Some may look weird,
Some may look threatening.
Yes, they are very questioning,
And not very welcoming,
Maybe they are menacing,
But do you think that's worth sentencing?

~

Yes, the sea is very exciting,
Even when the waves are maliciously fighting,
But the sea is worth more than just the boring old lighting,
And it will always be a surprising sighting.

Fears
Time: 18:18
Date: 31/1/2022

What is your fear?
Maybe you are scared of heights,
Maybe even teenagers,
It looks and feels scary, terrible and disturbing,
But why are you afraid? Scared and discouraged?

~

Scared of insects,
Scared of snakes,
What is it that makes you fret?
What makes you jump?
Hide, or cry?
Is this the thing that you'll be afraid of for the rest of your life?

~

You may not understand why it makes your skin crawl,
But you need to learn that you don't need to be afraid,
You need to understand that you are not alone,
Learn that you don't have to overcome your fears by yourself.

Birthdays
Time: 18:59
Date: 28/2/2022

How do you feel when you age every year?
Do you feel like you need a special meal?
Feeling like you have absolutely nothing to fear,
Do you feel that these are the time that things are getting real?

~

When your growing you change like your eyesight or hair,
Do you think that birthdays are the reason for the change in
your body?
Your skin and your wrinkles,
Your fractured back and how you might walk,
The momentous way that you change from child to adult,
The way that you see your life changing before your very eyes,

~

Birthdays happen every year, it's a cycle of some sort,
It marks the day that you were born, the day you came into this
world,
The day that you saw light, when you finally saw your mother's
face,
And when you opened your eyes to see the beginning of your
life,
You saw the happiness of your mother,
And how your life changed the lives of the people you love, in
just one expression.

The Seasons
<u>Time: 18:30</u>
<u>Date: 2/2/2022</u>

Spring, summer, autumn, and winter,
What is it they have in common?
It's not the turbulent weather of winter,
Or the scorching heat of summer,
They can be so different, just like humans in many ways.
But what are their differences? that's the million-dollar question.

~

The beautiful weather in spring,
The sultry weather in summer,
The breezy but cool air of autumn,
And the catastrophic wind of winter,
They can be so different, just like us in a way,
The best weather is most suited for our modern world.

~

Why is it that we pick favourites?
We experience each season every single year,
And we suffer the most on the coldest and hottest days,
We have the coldest winters and the hottest summers,
But have we ever asked ourselves the reason for this crisis?

Forgetting
Time: 17:55
Date: 8/2/2022

Sometimes you forget the things that don't seem important,
Like birthdays or feeding a pet,
The result of that may not look important,
But your heart and brain will determine that.

~

Forgetting to shower, forgetting to clean,
You'd think that it is easy when it's your normal hygiene,
Forgetting to wake up, forgetting family gatherings,
It can ruin both reputations,
And break the hearts of people who trusted you.

~

It may not seem important to you or to me,
But it may be important to someone else, and that's what we
don't see,
Trusting that you can do it is always going to be the key.
And later on in life, that will be something we all can agree.

Curiosity
Time: 16:57
Date: 10/2/2022

Are you curious?
Are you curious of death? What lies beyond?
Or what lies in this very book,
After so many times, you may just want it to disappear,
In this life of curiosity, it's a time for mistakes.

~

Having curiosity is natural, it'll happen throughout your life,
It can lead you into places you don't want to be in,
And turn your life into a world of trouble,
Between you and your curiosity, who do you think would win?
Because after so long, trust would evaporate.

~

Curiosity may not be an excuse, but there's something that
causes it,
Ignorance, yes, you read that correctly,
Human's lack of knowledge, the thing that makes us all
different,
Ignorance can be caused because of curiosity,
But curiosity doesn't always justify ignorance.

My Inspiration
Time: 16:42
Date: 15/2/2022

My inspiration, the reason for this book,
May not be a mystery to all,
The thing that is most special to me,
And the thing that gives me hope for my future.

~

My inspiration could be many things,
Like a person on the internet,
Or a role model in my life,
As times have changed, they've seen what I can do,
My worst and my best,
And how I've changed since I was little.

~

My role model is my mother,
My own flesh and blood,
But she is not the only one that gives me inspiration.

~

My teacher, my friends,
The people that keep me sane,
They've been with me on my journey,
And they give me hope, that their life will never end.

Confidence is something that many people do and do not have,
Confidence is something that makes you believe in yourself.
No matter the problem,
Some people lack this important trait,
Which may develop a hole in their heart.

~

After only so many years, you could get used to it,
You believe so many things that are not true,
And believe that you going to fail, even if you don't,
And the confidence that you once had, will be turned into
smoke.

~

Your confidence is always there, you just need to believe,
Many people think they'll fail, but could accomplish much
more,
All you need is to believe, and you could do something amazing,
Not everyone will believe in you, so you need to believe in your-
self.

Think Like the Person You Want to Become
Time: 17:26
Date: 15/2/2022

Any job you want to have, you need to train for,
If that's learning anatomy, or strengthening your vocal cords,
Whatever it is, it's important for your career,
But you shouldn't only act like someone you want to become;
you should think like them.

~

Trying to be someone you're not, doesn't get you anywhere,
Do something you love, cherish and care about,
It doesn't matter how easy or difficult it is,
The only thing that matters is how much you help the people
that you love.

~

You need to be kind and understanding to be a doctor,
And learn that not everyone will like you if you want to be a
singer,
But it's the thought that will count,
And the amount of lives you would have changed because you
think like the person you want to become.

Feeling Invisible
<u>**Time: 18:52**</u>
<u>**Date: 28/2/2022**</u>

Do you feel invisible?
Do you feel that the people around you don't see you?
Well, I sometimes do too,
But it's normal to feel this way,
I'm here to show you how that can feel,
And how it can affect you mentally.

~

You can feel that nobody cares, that nobody can see you,
That nobody speaks and looks at you like everyone else,
Maybe that the people you used to love, who you trusted the
most,
Have betrayed you and turned into your enemy.

~

You may feel lonely, there's nobody you can speak to,
You feel that there's nobody to turn to, that nobody would
understand,
That you are alone on this earth, and that you feel empty inside.
That everyone detests you, no matter how hard you try.

~

But maybe you're wrong, and that the opposite is happening,
Everyone can see you, everyone can speak to you,
They too can feel alone on this earth,

They can feel that there's nobody to turn to,
But with the amount of people on this earth, with the people
they can contact,
Is that really true?

Perfection
<ins>Time: 18:25</ins>
<ins>Date: 15/2/2022</ins>

No one is perfect, perfection is for no one,
So many people think they're flawed and imperfect,
But everyone is flawed, even if they seem like they're not,
As it's not about what's on the outside, but on the inside.

~

For so many years people think that there is no one better,
No one can beat them even if they tried,
But that's not true, life is not always what it seems,
As on the inside people are not the same,
And our flesh is just a covering.

~

It's hard to believe that everyone's imperfect, even for me.
Everyone thinks and believes something that's untrue about
themselves.
That could be, big lips, small ears, even being skinny or large,
They find that there is always someone who look better,
But even then, they need to understand that they're not the only
one that's flawed,
The whole human race is not perfect, and that's something we
need to accept.

Contagious Love
Time: 18:40
Date: 15/2/2022

Contagious love, what exactly is it?
It's the love that spreads like wildfire,
The love that makes you believe that you could do anything,
The love that everyone should experience.

~

When you truly love someone, it feels like you're the only ones
on the planet,
But when love is in the air, it takes hold of many,
And when you're with your significant other,
You want to stop time to be with them for the rest of your life.

~

It blows my mind, that people feel alone,
But that's not always true,
The people you love, will love you back,
And even sickness, or in a bad mood, they will take care of you,
And they will forever understand that you'd do the same for
them.

You could have a commitment to reading, or a relationship,
But it's not just something you can easily equip,
You need to act like it's your own flesh and blood,
Before your life can go crashing with a thud.

~

If it's really important, than you need to care,
Don't just look at responsibilities and glare,
Because it will live in your lifestyle, you'll never forget it,
An in the end when it truly matters, you'll never quit.

~

Things that are important, will include things like this,
And when you get the reward, it'll feel like bliss,
It's not just about the difficulties, but it's about the ending,
It's about how you saved someone from descending.

Every Journey is Different
Time: 17:27
Date: 16/2/2022

Every life is different, no matter how long, short, or spontaneous
it is,
The life that we live could seem weird or disgusting,
Because there are so many eyes to judge and to contradict,
But just like your life, they are so different than many other
people.

~

So many people are experiencing different things,
And they love and hate things that are different than you,
They act differently, if that's good or bad,
But it's not just what's on the outside, but on the inside too.

~

Everyone's appearance is different, but in this world is that really
important?
Everyone's heart is different, but why is it that some hearts are
shrivelled?

~

The journey to an education,
The journey to exploring,
The journey to another country,
The journey to lose weight,
It all sounds so easy, but the experience can be much harder,

It can cause pain like a pregnancy,
Or go unnoticeable, like the digestive system.

Positive Things
Time: 17:44
Date: 16/2/2022

Positive things, is one of the only things that keeps us going,
In our lives, positive things help support us,
And help us to think that we're worth it,
But good things don't always come out of thin air,
And our lives can't always be dependent of someone.

~

In our lives, responsibilities will overcome you, and wreak havoc
on your sanity,
But we need to learn that good things don't just happen when
you want it to,
And depression can leave your head blank with horrible
thoughts,
And will leave a mark in our minds.

~

Good things don't just happen to good people, they too need to
work for it,
And when you're in your darkest moments, your mind has to be
your best friend,
Because when you think positive, and you train for what you
think is important,
Your dream will become a reality, and it will congratulate you,
And say, that your work was worth it.

Overthinking Leads to Sadness
Time: 18:06
Date: 16/2/2022

After so many times, after so many years, you'd think that we
would have stopped,
Over thinking leads to sadness, which means quite a lot.

~

If the things that makes you happy, takes a toll on your body
and allows you to stress,
Then taking a break would seem to be the best,
But many times, people don't think that's a solution,
And this can lead to a dark cloud, which hangs over their heads,
and make them a mess.

~

The best things to ever happen, always have a backstory,
But when they are so important to you, they can lead to
overthinking,
Overthinking can lead to horrible thoughts, that you'll think
will come alive,
And lead your hairs to stand still, like sharp prickly trees.

~

Negative thoughts can affect you more than you think,
And when they do, they scream and claw at the things you love,
They can make you paranoid and scared,

But when you truly believe that you can do it, you will feel lifted by hope.
And believe that you could achieve your dreams, just like The Pope.

What Goes Around Comes Around
Time: 18:33
Date: 2/3/2022

What goes around comes around, have you ever heard that
before?
Bullying and stealing, yeah, this involves that too,
Karma can be a menace, but some people seem to have no clue.

~

Helping the poor and being kind,
Sometimes there's good karma that you can find.
Being kind and being good,
Doing nice things, doesn't depend on your childhood.
Helping the people you love and support,
Can change people's lives, but that's not something we always
report.

~

Good or bad, naughty or nice,
It can all be so easy, like cooking some rice,
Sometimes it's hard, we all make mistakes,
But we should treat people how we want to be treated, for every-
one's sake,
Because when you're in their shoes,
You would know how it would feel to lose.

The Past Cannot be Changed
Time: 16: 20
Date: 17/2/2022

Our past is the thing that gives us knowledge,
And makes us memorise our mistakes,
But our mistakes sometimes are important to acknowledge,
When you forget that bones, aren't the only things that breaks.

~

Pain and regret, that can cause scars,
You'd think that it would just disappear, like the explosion of
stars,
It can cause trauma and change your mentality,
And can even break you down and cause a fatality,
People don't understand that your past can cause pain,
Because it will always be embedded in your brain.

~

You cannot change things like words or giving birth,
As your memories will remain in your mind, until you leave this
earth,
You can have regrets and change, as life goes on,
But you have to learn how to change your life, and with this you
have won.

Judging Others
Time: 16:46
Date: 17/2/2022

Never judge others,
We all bleed the same colour blood.

~

We all have bones,
We all have a brain,
We all have blood running through our veins.

~

When you judge others, what really do you gain?
You judge them when they are disabled,
You judge the colour of their skin,
You judge their partners,
Even their next of kin.

~

After years of bullying, your understanding of life can become
paper thin,
You can be tall, short, or even going to the gym,
Still, bullies can judge and make your feelings spin,
But even after this, you can reign supreme, and then really feel
like you can win.

Happiness is Within
Time: 17:23
Date: 17/2/2022

I know that I can find happiness within me,
Even if I'm pushed, shoved, and thrown out into the sea.

~

I will do things that makes me happy,
Even if others don't agree,
They can bound me, tie me up
But my heart will forever be free.

~

I will live my life,
Even if that means, I am stabbed by a knife,
I can still stay free with happiness and love,
And feel that I can fly like a dove.

~

I will feel the sensation of knowing I'm loved,
But most importantly, by everyone above,
And that one day, I can fit in the clouds like a glove.

Kindness is Free
<u>Time: 18:14</u>
<u>Date: 17/2/2022</u>

Kindness is free, it isn't worth a thing,
Negativity, is what bullies bring,
Bullies are horrible, but kindness is the king,
After so long, it's agreed that kindness is better than anything.

~

If you see someone having a bad time,
You should help them, kindness isn't a crime,
Kindness is infinite, you can even do it at lunchtime,
It can be really easy; feelings isn't something you have to mime.

~

We've learnt that kindness is reliable, free and easy,
That feeling for someone to be nice, when you're uneasy,
You understand that you just made someone day a little better,
And they'd do the same for you, even if it's giving you cuddles,
through a very big sweater.

Things Can Change Overtime
<u>Time: 18:38</u>
<u>Date: 17/2/2022</u>

Things can change, but only if you try,
Attempts can be made, even If that means you will cry,
But it'll all be worth it, as your end product will be your reward,
And you trying your best alone, will be adored.

~

Things can only be different if you change,
And although the journey may seem strange,
It's best to try, rather than giving up altogether,
But nothing should get in your way, not even walking through bad weather,
Being confident is better than anxiety crawling up your back,
Understanding that you can do it, makes confidence stack.

~

Trying your hardest and failing is just fine,
But giving up immediately, isn't a good sign,
Confidence can run low, but the people you love can help you along the way,
Because it doesn't matter how you feel, they will always stay.

Smiles Are Contagious
Time: 19:51
Date: 2/3/2022

Smiles are the things that keep us running wild,
When you can be having a horrible day, smiles will make you feel
okay,
Funny things and friends, it can all make you and your sadness
make amends,
It can make you happy in an instant, and find that you smile
too,
As smiles can brighten your day,
And you know the experience when it's happening to you.

~

You can start your day, with a smile and happiness,
Because at times we all feel disheartened and weak,
You can be filled with sadness, and a smile will add a spring in
your step,
As a bad day can be changed with a simple gesture,
Smiling may be simple, but the way we treat others isn't.

~

Your mood can be changed in an instant,
You can smile for so long; everyone can see it from a distance.

You Only Fail if You Quit
Time: 19:08
Date: 21/2/2022

You'll only ever fail, if you quit,
It's like going to the gym, trying to get fit,
If you don't keep up the hard work,
You'll have a fat armpit,
So, it's best to stay focused and keep working at it.

~

So, let's stop for a minute and think about our education,
It can look difficult and overcome you with frustration,
Some say the best thing about it is the celebration,
But it's so much more than that and can be as easy as a conversation.

~

Education can be interesting, it can fill you with captivation,
It's the demonstration to have the ability to teach others in rotation.
We are talking about that time, when you've achieved so much, it was almost time for your graduation,
To have the mental capacity, to build a foundation.

~

It's time to dig up those bad seeds, re-plant, rebuild, take your pens out and feel the sensation,
Let your seeds adapt, attract, then change your location.

~

When you think about quitting,
It can burn into your blood until you feel the temptation,
The temptation to work harder, the temptation to succeed,
The temptation for knowledge,
But not the temptation for greed.

The end,
At least for now.......

Ingram Content Group UK Ltd.
Milton Keynes UK
UKHW020608130323
418477UK00011B/1858

9 781916 871595